PENNSYLVANIA

HELLO
U.S.A.

by Gwenyth Swain

Lerner Publications Company

You'll find this picture of mountain laurel at the beginning of each chapter. The mountain laurel (Kalmia latifolia) *is an evergreen shrub that generally has white or pink flowers. Found in eastern North America, it is the state flower of both Pennsylvania and Connecticut.*

Cover (left): Amish boys in Lancaster County. Cover (right): The Liberty Bell in Philadelphia. Pages 2–3: Cemetery Hill at Gettysburg Battlefield. Page 3: Pittsburgh skyline.

This book is available in two editions:
Library binding by Lerner Publications Company, a division of Lerner Publishing Group
Soft cover by First Avenue Editions, an imprint of Lerner Publishing Group
241 First Avenue North
Minneapolis, MN 55401 U.S.A.

Website address: www.lernerbooks.com

Library of Congress Cataloging-in-Publication Data

Swain, Gwenyth, 1961–
    Pennsylvania / by Gwenyth Swain (Rev. and expanded 2nd ed.)
      p.   cm. — (Hello U.S.A.)
    Includes index.
    ISBN: 0–8225–4061–4 (lib. bdg. : alk. paper)
    ISBN: 0–8225–4147–5 (pbk. : alk. paper)
    1. Pennsylvania—Juvenile literature. [1. Pennsylvania.] I. Title. II. Series.
F149.3 .S93 2002
974.8—dc21   2001001740

Manufactured in the United States of America
1 2 3 4 5 6 – JR – 07 06 05 04 03 02

CONTENTS

Wildflowers thrive in the mountainous forests of northeastern Pennsylvania.

THE LAND

From Lowlands to Mountains

 f you want to travel around Pennsylvania, just hop on a highway. Pennsylvania is the place where big highways got their start. Back in 1940, travelers began driving on a section of Pennsylvania's **turnpike,** a four-lane toll road and the nation's first modern highway.

The turnpike crosses the state from east to west. This and other roads link Pennsylvania to its neighbors. Pennsylvania is bordered by New York to the north, New Jersey to the east, Delaware and Maryland to the south, West Virginia to the southwest, and Ohio to the west. Lake Erie touches on Pennsylvania's northwest corner.

Trucks cruise along the Pennsylvania Turnpike.

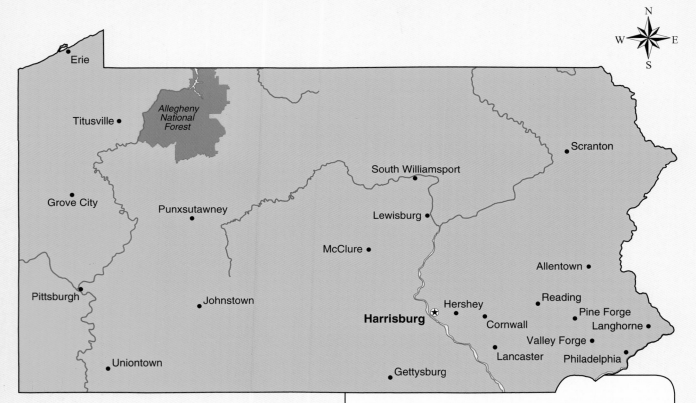

Erie •

Titusville •

Allegheny National Forest

Grove City •

Punxsutawney •

Scranton •

South Williamsport •

Lewisburg •

McClure •

Allentown •

Pittsburgh •

Johnstown •

Harrisburg ⭐

Hershey •

Reading •

Cornwall •

Pine Forge •
Langhorne •

Valley Forge •

Lancaster •

Philadelphia •

Uniontown •

Gettysburg •

N
W   E
S

PENNSYLVANIA
Political Map

⭐ State capital

0	20	40 Miles

0	20	40	60	80 Kilometers

The drawing of Pennsylvania on this page is called a political map. It shows features created by people, including cities, railways, and parks. The map on the facing page is called a physical map. It shows physical features of Pennsylvania, such as coasts, islands, mountains, rivers, and lakes. The colors represent a range of elevations, or heights above sea level (see legend box). This map also shows the geographical regions of Pennsylvania.

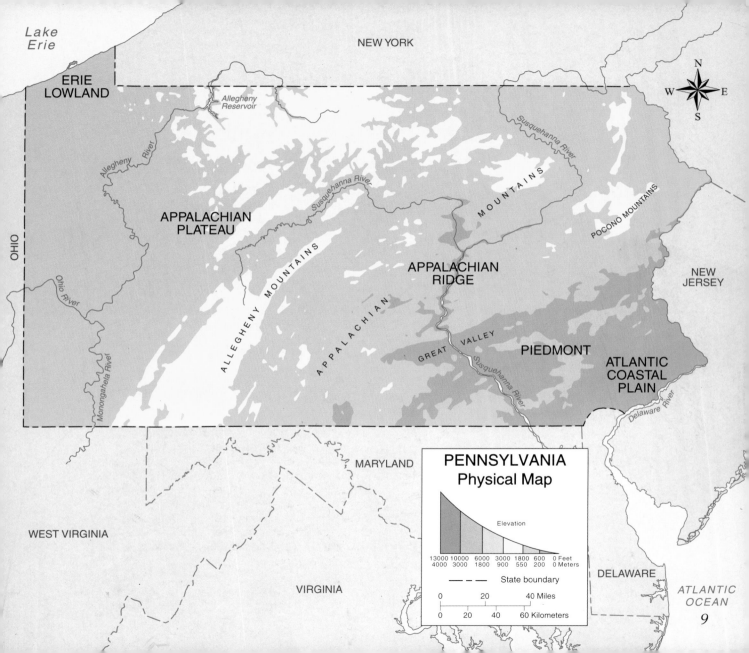

Lake Erie

NEW YORK

ERIE LOWLAND

Allegheny Reservoir

Allegheny River

Susquehanna River

OHIO

APPALACHIAN PLATEAU

Susquehanna River

A L L E G H E N Y   M O U N T A I N S

M O U N T A I N S

Pocono Mountains

POCONO MOUNTAINS

Ohio River

APPALACHIAN RIDGE

A P P A L A C H I A N

NEW JERSEY

Monongahela River

GREAT   VALLEY

PIEDMONT

Susquehanna River

ATLANTIC COASTAL PLAIN

Delaware River

MARYLAND

WEST VIRGINIA

VIRGINIA

DELAWARE

ATLANTIC OCEAN

PENNSYLVANIA
Physical Map

Elevation

| 13000 | 10000 | 6000 | 3000 | 1800 | 600 | 0 Feet |
| 4000 | 3000 | 1800 | 900 | 550 | 200 | 0 Meters |

- - - State boundary

| 0 | 20 | 40 Miles |

| 0 | 20 | 40 | 60 Kilometers |

9

Pennsylvania's mountains look like rolling, green hills from a hang glider's point of view.

Mountains are the most important feature in the state's landscape. Pennsylvania's mountains are all part of the Appalachians, which began forming millions of years ago. From the mountains, the land slopes downward to rolling hills and lowlands.

Located in the middle of the Mid-Atlantic region of the United States, Pennsylvania has five major land regions. The Appalachian Plateau covers most of western and northern Pennsylvania. Broad-topped mountains, called plateaus, include the Allegheny and Pocono ranges of the Appalachian Mountains.

Trains wind their way through the mountains near Johnstown, in southwestern Pennsylvania, whizzing down steep tracks and across bridges.

The Appalachian Plateau holds a big share of the state's natural resources. The world's first successful oil well was drilled in the region in Titusville in 1859. Rich veins of coal have also been found and mined in the plateau region.

East of the Appalachian Plateau is the Appalachian Ridge, a region of steep, narrow mountain peaks and many valleys. Grouped together, a number of these valleys make up the Great Valley. Stretching from eastern Pennsylvania to the Maryland border, the Great Valley is famous for its fertile farmland.

Farming is also important in the Piedmont region in southeastern Pennsylvania. The Piedmont's rolling land attracted many German and Swiss farmers, nicknamed the Pennsylvania Dutch, in the 1600s.

The Piedmont region in the southeastern part of the state is blanketed with farmland.

Pennsylvania's smallest regions—the Atlantic Coastal Plain and the Erie Lowland—are both close to water. Part of a region that extends to the Atlantic Ocean, the coastal plain is a strip of lowland in the Delaware River Valley.

The coastal plain is home to Philadelphia, the state's largest city and its first major port. Ships from Philadelphia reach the Atlantic Ocean by traveling south on the Delaware River.

In northwestern Pennsylvania, the Erie Lowland hugs the southern shore of Lake Erie, one of the **Great Lakes.** From the port city of Erie, Pennsylvania's products travel to other cities on the Great Lakes and beyond.

A brilliant red sunset reflects off Lake Erie. This lake borders the northwestern part of Pennsylvania.

Hikers stop near the capital city of Harrisburg to enjoy this spectacular view of the Susquehanna River.

Most of Lake Erie is located outside Pennsylvania's borders. Inside the state are several large lakes, including the Allegheny Reservoir, an artificial lake in the Allegheny National Forest. Northeastern Pennsylvania is dotted with small lakes.

Rivers were the best travel routes in Pennsylvania before highways and turnpikes were built. Two of Pennsylvania's biggest rivers, the Allegheny and the Monongahela, join at Pittsburgh to form the Ohio River. The Susquehanna River meanders through the central part of the state, while the Delaware River marks Pennsylvania's eastern border.

Forests, like the Allegheny National Forest in northern Pennsylvania, cover much of the state.

About three-fifths of Pennsylvania is covered with forest. Hickory, oak, and walnut trees thrive in southern Pennsylvania. Black bears live in the lush woods of northern Pennsylvania, while ruffed grouse are found along woodland streams. Deer, muskrats, rabbits, and raccoons are common throughout the state.

Bears are native to Pennsylvania's many forests.

The state's climate and rainfall help trees and other plants grow. Pennsylvania averages 41 inches of rain and other forms of **precipitation** each year.

Summers in Pennsylvania are warm, and winters are chilly but not bitterly cold. The average January temperature is 27° F. In July temperatures rise to an average of 71° F.

From tree-covered mountain plateaus to rolling farmland to busy ports, Pennsylvania has a lot to offer. Whether you travel the turnpike or the back roads, the state is sure to surprise you.

The Keystone State

People have lived in Pennsylvania for over 12,000 years. About 15,000 Native Americans were living in the area when Europeans first arrived in the 1600s. These Native Americans belonged to several different groups.

The Lenape made their homes in the broad valley of the Delaware River and were called Delawares by European settlers. The Susquehannocks, or "people of a well-watered land," lived along the Susquehanna River. The Monongahela lived in the west near the Ohio, Allegheny, and Monongahela Rivers.

People have lived in the "well-watered land" of Pennsylvania for about 12,000 years.

All of these groups lived mainly by farming. Corn, beans, and squash—all of which grew easily in river valleys—were major crops. Native Americans also harvested sap from maple trees.

To add to their diet and to provide skins for clothing, the Native Americans hunted deer, bears, and other animals. Fishing was also an important activity.

In 1609 British explorer Henry Hudson took a ship up the Delaware River and became the first European to meet the Lenape. Hudson worked for a Dutch fur-trading company.

This colorful painting portrays a Native American leader speaking to his fellow Lenape. The Lenape lived in the Delaware River Valley.

Most of the Europeans who followed Hudson in the early 1600s were fur traders. In the 1630s, the Dutch set up trading posts near the Lenape on the western shores of the Delaware River. Swedish settlers soon followed. The Dutch and Swedes traded pots, guns, and cloth for furs from animals hunted by Native Americans.

By the 1640s, Dutch and Swedish settlers were arguing over control of the Delaware River Valley. The Swedes had formed a **colony,** or settlement, called New Sweden near what later became Philadelphia. In 1655 Dutch soldiers seized New Sweden. The struggle between the Dutch and the Swedes continued until 1664, when the British took control of the area.

People in Europe watched the settlers' progress with interest. William Penn of Great Britain thought the Delaware Valley would be a good place to live and farm. Penn was a follower of George Fox. In the mid-1600s, Fox started a religious movement called the Society of Friends, or Quakers. Friends believed in equality and in freedom of worship.

William Penn founded Pennsylvania to create a place where Quakers and others could freely practice their religion. The colony, however, was named after Penn's father. The name's ending—sylvania—means "woods."

Penn dreamed of a new home where Friends and others could practice their religion freely. Pennsylvania was to be such a place.

On March 4, 1681, King Charles II of Britain gave Penn control of land west of the Delaware River. The king owed Penn's father a great deal of money. By granting land to William Penn, the king got rid of a large debt and a group of people he considered religious troublemakers.

Many Friends moved to the new colony of Pennsylvania, settling mainly in the Delaware

Native Americans of the Delaware River Valley traded with Swedish settlers.

Valley. German and Swiss people of the Amish and Mennonite faiths soon followed, attracted by good farmland and religious freedom. Scottish and Irish settlers also helped the colony's population grow.

William Penn and the Lenape Indians held talks at a meeting that might have resembled this one. This painting was made by Quaker artist Edward Hicks.

Penn, the Lenape, and Peace

The Lenape made wampum belts from strings of shell beads. The belts were considered sacred. Anyone holding a wampum belt was expected to tell the truth. According to legend, Lenape leader Tamanend gave a wampum belt to William Penn in 1682 to celebrate a treaty, or agreement. On the belt given to Penn, two figures—one Lenape and one European—hold hands.

Penn and later colonists continued to meet with and buy land from Native Americans. Most of the land that later became Pennsylvania was purchased from the Native Americans by 1768. Over the years, more European settlers arrived and Pennsylvania's Native American population declined. Many Native Americans moved west, looking for better hunting grounds, and many others died from European diseases.

In this painting, the French fight the British in what became known as the French and Indian War.

Penn and other settlers got along well with their Native American neighbors. But as more Europeans arrived in the region, the Native Americans' homelands became smaller and more crowded.

In 1754 the British and French argued over who would control North America. Many Native Americans joined forces with the French against the British in what became known as the French and Indian War.

During the 1750s, this "Join, or Die" cartoon snake was printed to encourage colonists to stick together during the French and Indian War. The sections of the snake stand for the colonies. The snake image was used again in the 1770s to rally the colonies against Great Britain.

Pennsylvania was a British colony, so most colonists sided with Great Britain. When the war ended, the British had won control over large parts of North America, including what later became Pennsylvania. The conflict, which lasted nearly 10 years, marked the end of peaceful relations between Native Americans and Europeans.

To pay for the war, Great Britain set high taxes on goods going to and from its colonies in North America. Many people in Pennsylvania and the other colonies were angered. They felt they were being treated unfairly.

In 1774 representatives from the colonies gathered together in Philadelphia for a meeting they called the First Continental Congress. The colonists drew up a list of complaints against the British. They called for an end to unfair taxes and decided to stop trading with Great Britain.

British troops attacked the colonists in April 1775 to try to force them to stop their protests. At first it seemed that the two sides might reach a settlement. But when the Second Continental Congress met in Philadelphia in May, the colonies voted to fight for independence from Great Britain.

Members of the Second Continental Congress signed the Declaration of Independence at Independence Hall in Philadelphia. The U.S. Constitution was written there later.

On July 4, 1776, about a year after the American War of Independence had begun, the Continental Congress passed the Declaration of Independence. In the declaration, 13 colonies officially claimed to be independent of Great Britain. They were forming a new, free country, whether the British liked it or not.

But the British did not intend to lose the colonies. In September 1777, at the Battle of Brandywine near Philadelphia, British redcoats surrounded the Continental Army, led by General George Washington. The British took Philadelphia, and the Continental Army was lucky to get out alive.

The cracked Liberty Bell in Philadelphia has become a well-known symbol of freedom. According to legend, the bell was rung on July 4, 1776, to proclaim the independence of the colonies.

Washington and his soldiers were still smarting from their defeat when they settled in for the winter at Valley Forge, northwest of Philadelphia. Food soon ran short. Then smallpox broke out. Some of the men deserted and others died, but the Continental Army held together. The long, hard winter made the soldiers even more determined to fight on.

These huts at Valley Forge are replicas of the huts that Washington and his soldiers used during the American War of Independence.

27

During the war, Pennsylvania's farmers grew grain to feed soldiers and horses. American troops, including many from Pennsylvania, used gunpowder from the colony's factories.

By the time the colonists had defeated the British in 1783, Pennsylvania's key role in the war had earned it the nickname Keystone. The wedge-shaped keystone at the top of an arch holds the arch together. Pennsylvania helped hold the colonies together during the revolution.

In 1787 representatives from the former British colonies came to Philadelphia to write their new nation's **constitution,** or laws. Pennsylvania was the second state to ratify, or approve, the Constitution of the United States of America.

Pennsylvania was the richest state in the country. Farmers there grew grain for milling into flour. Miners in northeastern Pennsylvania dug coal, while workers in Scranton and other growing cities made more iron than in any other state in the Union.

With 42,000 people in 1790, Philadelphia was the nation's largest city. The port of Philadelphia

Settlers heading west traveled in Conestoga wagons. The wagon was invented in Pennsylvania in the 1790s.

was also the first stop for many **immigrants,** or settlers from other countries.

Some immigrants found jobs in textile and flour mills along Philadelphia's rivers. Immigrants looking for less crowded land generally headed to Pittsburgh, a gateway to the American frontier. Pioneers stocked up on supplies at Pittsburgh's busy stores and then traveled west by wagon or river barge.

Settlers and other travelers often found it hard to get from one part of the state to another because of a lack of roads. Merchants and manufacturers also wished for easier routes across the state, especially over the steep mountains of central Pennsylvania.

In the mid-1800s, passengers in canal boats had an interesting way of getting over the Allegheny Mountains to Johnstown. They and their boats were loaded onto railcars that took them over the mountains.

In the early 1800s, miles of roads and many new bridges were built in the state. Canals linked Philadelphia and Pittsburgh by 1834. Travel between eastern and western Pennsylvania was made even easier when railroads crossed the mountains in the 1850s.

A different kind of railroad, called the **Underground Railroad,** brought a number of African Americans to the Keystone State from the early to mid-1800s. This railroad had no cars or tracks. Instead it was the name for a secret system of routes taking slaves from the South to freedom in the North.

In towns like Pine Forge, Grove City, and Lewisburg, "conductors" worked on Pennsylvania's Underground Railroad. These volunteers hid, fed, and helped find safe passage for hundreds of slaves escaping to freedom.

Slavery was dividing the country. Owning people was illegal in Pennsylvania and other Northern states. Many Pennsylvanians thought slavery was wrong.

In 1860 Southern states began withdrawing from the Union to form the Confederacy, a separate nation where slavery was legal. By 1861 tensions between the Confederacy and the Union led to war.

Pennsylvania stood behind the Union throughout the Civil War. Ironworkers supplied the Union army with guns and ammunition. Philadelphia's bankers loaned the Union money to fight the war. Textile workers wove cloth for uniforms. And Pennsylvanians from all parts of the state lost their lives in battle.

As a conductor on the Underground Railroad, William Still aided many fleeing slaves on the road to freedom. Still was from Philadelphia.

31

The Battle of Gettysburg, in south central Pennsylvania, was the most deadly battle waged in the state. Between the first and third of July 1863, more than 50,000 men were wounded or killed in what was called the Most Terrible Struggle of the War.

The Confederate army lost as many as 28,000 men at Gettysburg. With such heavy losses, the Confederates no longer had enough soldiers to lead major attacks. For the Union, Gettysburg was the turning point in the war. By 1865 the Confederacy had been defeated.

Pennsylvania's soldiers *(above)* fought for the Union during the Civil War. The Battle of Gettysburg *(right)*

Water, Water, Everywhere

Johnstown, in southwestern Pennsylvania, was like many of the state's growing cities in the late 1800s. Workers crowded into Johnstown, and factories seemed to have jobs for everyone. But while the city grew, a terrible danger lay in the mountains nearby.

Johnstown is in a deep valley at the meeting place of the Little Conemaugh River and Stony Creek. People there were

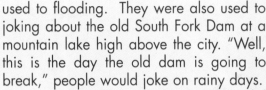

used to flooding. They were also used to joking about the old South Fork Dam at a mountain lake high above the city. "Well, this is the day the old dam is going to break," people would joke on rainy days.

On May 31, 1889, the dam did break. Water streaming through the broken dam hit Johnstown so fast that it picked up trees and train cars and tossed them in the air.

Over 2,000 men, women, and children died in the flood and in a great fire that raged in the wreckage of houses trapped against a bridge. In about 10 minutes, nearly all of Johnstown was destroyed or underwater.

When it was all over, the people of Johnstown were stunned. They rebuilt their city and faced high water and floods again in later years. But none has ever matched the power and destruction of the 1889 Johnstown Flood.

This picture of a house after the Johnstown flood shows the devastation caused by the flood.

Workers at the Homestead steelworks near Pittsburgh produced 25,000 tons of steel monthly throughout the 1890s.

After the Civil War, Pennsylvanians set about meeting the needs of the nation. High-quality coal was discovered in western Pennsylvania, and miners found jobs digging it out. Mills sprang up in Pittsburgh, using coal power to make steel for railroads, machinery, and bridge supports. By the late 1800s, Pennsylvania was leading the country in manufacturing and mining.

Pittsburgh and other cities in Pennsylvania had so many jobs that immigrants came there by the thousands. Leaving homes in Hungary, Poland, Russia, Ukraine, and other parts of Europe, most immigrants worked in Pennsylvania's mines, mills, and factories.

Life for workers in Pennsylvania during the late 1800s wasn't easy, especially for the many young people forced to work. When families couldn't make ends meet, children went out to work—often for as many as 60 hours per week.

At that time, it was against the law for anyone under the age of 12 to have a job in the Keystone State. But more children worked in Pennsylvania than in any other state in the Union.

Pennsylvania's coal mine companies employed young boys to work in breakers—unheated rooms outside coal mines. The boys picked shale out of pieces of coal.

Many people throughout the United States became unemployed during the Great Depression. These men gathered in a Philadelphia park to trade stories and job leads.

Many young Pennsylvanians continued to work long hours until the 1930s, when jobs were hard for anyone—young or old—to find. This period of hard times, from 1929 to about 1939, is called the Great Depression. During the depression, businesses and banks closed, and people lost their jobs. As wages fell, even people who had jobs found it difficult to get by.

The depression ended when the country entered the Second World War in 1941. During the war, more than 1 million Pennsylvanians served in the armed forces. Many jobs were created, and Pennsylvanians made warships, uniforms, and chocolate bars for soldiers.

The first stretch of the Pennsylvania Turnpike opened in 1940. Cars lined up right away to try out the highway.

When the war ended in 1945, many former soldiers were hired to work in Pennsylvania's factories. New highways such as the Pennsylvania Turnpike made it easier to send goods to other states.

Since the 1950s, Pennsylvania has been a state of both problems and promise. In 1979 a serious accident took place at Three Mile Island, near the city of Harrisburg. Three Mile Island is a plant that uses **nuclear power** to generate electricity.

Pittsburgh, the state's second largest city, has made progress toward a cleaner environment.

During the accident, a small amount of dangerous **radioactive** gas escaped. The power plant was contaminated and had to be shut down for cleanup.

While such problems grab headlines in newspapers across the country, Pennsylvanians take pride in the many promising changes in their state. For example, Pittsburgh, once called Smoky City because of pollution, was ranked one of the best places to live in the country in the 1980s. With its clean air and water, Pittsburgh shows the promise of Pennsylvania's future.

In the 1990s, Pennsylvania preserved and restored many of its historic sites, attracting visitors and jobs to Philadelphia and Pittsburgh. The state continues to produce steel, but the economy is shifting from manufacturing to financial, educational, and other service industries.

Industrial Giant

ittsburgh in the west and Philadelphia in the east are the two biggest cities in the Keystone State, but there's more than just a turnpike in between. Fascinating places and people can be found in every corner of the state.

Pennsylvania's population is big and diverse. With nearly 12.3 million people, the state has the sixth largest population in the country.

A statue of Pennsylvania's founder, William Penn, looks out over downtown Philadelphia from atop city hall.

Pennsylvania is home to Mennonites and Amish, people who choose to live in a traditional manner.

Native Americans were once the only people in the area. About 84 percent of Pennsylvanians are white people of European backgrounds. African Americans make up nearly 10 percent of the state's population. About 3 percent of Pennsylvanians are **Latinos** (people with Latin American roots). Asian Americans make up about 2 percent of Pennsylvania's population, and Native Americans number about 0.1 percent.

Philadelphia is the largest city in the state. It is home to people of many different ethnic backgrounds. With more than 1.5 million residents, Philadelphia easily tops Pittsburgh, which has about 335,000 people. Other big cities in Pennsylvania include Erie, Allentown, Reading, Upper Darby, and Scranton.

The town of Hershey, Pennsylvania, is the perfect place for chocolate lovers of any age. Hershey has the world's largest chocolate factory, an amusement park, and a museum that tells the history of Hershey's chocolate. The town even has street lamps shaped like chocolate kisses!

About 15 percent of working Pennsylvanians are employed in manufacturing. Many of the biggest steel companies in the country are located in the Keystone State, but steel isn't the only thing Pennsylvanians produce.

At food-processing companies such as H. J. Heinz in Pittsburgh, people make everything from ketchup to baby food. Candy makers at the world's largest chocolate factory in Hershey, Pennsylvania, produce tons of chocolate bars.

In Philadelphia at the University of Pennsylvania, researchers built the first general-purpose computer in 1946. Workers in the Philadelphia area continue to turn out computers and information systems.

Government employees work in the Harrisburg capitol building *(left)* and in surrounding buildings. Coal mining continues to be important in Pennsylvania. This worker *(below)* drills a hole for explosives.

Though many Native Americans and early European settlers farmed the land, only 2 percent of Pennsylvanians work in agriculture. The state's farmers keep busy raising livestock and dairy cattle and by growing mushrooms, corn, and hay.

With its rich deposits of coal, Pennsylvania has had a long history of mining. Since the 1950s, however, many of Pennsylvania's coal mines have shut down, as other fuels have become more popular. Fewer than 1 percent of the state's workers are miners.

About two-thirds of the people in Pennsylvania have service jobs, in which they work helping people and businesses. Service workers staff hospitals, run banks, and meet the needs of tourists. About 10 percent of Pennsylvanians work for the government. Many of them work in Harrisburg, the state capital.

Products from dairy cows make up a small but vital portion of Pennsylvania's economy.

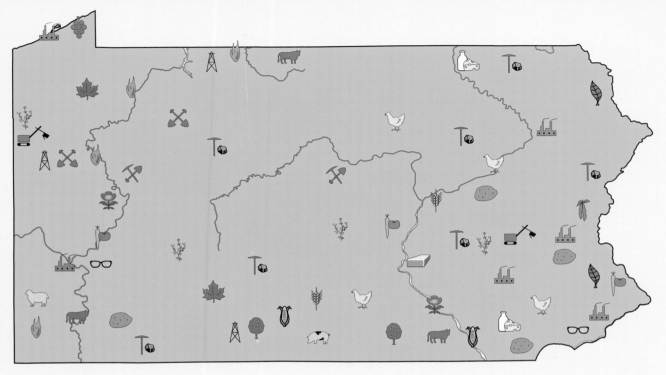

PENNSYLVANIA
Economic Map

The symbols on this map show where different economic activities take place in Pennsylvania. The legend below explains what each symbol stands for.

Beef cattle	Dairy products	Iron ore	Natural gas	Poultry	Stone
Clay	Fruit	Manufacturing	Oats	Sheep	Tobacco
Coal	Grapes	Maple syrup	Oil	Silver	Tourism
Corn	Hogs	Nursery products	Potatoes	Soybeans	Vegetables
					Wheat

The annual Mummers' Parade in Philadelphia brings a variety of dressed-up band members and dancers to the streets.

It's easy to see why tourists visit Pennsylvania when you take a look at what's going on in the Keystone State. On New Year's Day, costumed Philadelphians take to the streets in the Mummers' Parade. The parade's roots combine German and African American traditions of greeting the new year. Mummers entertain the crowds with their music, fancy dancing, and big, bright costumes.

In Pittsburgh, people celebrate the arts with the Three Rivers Arts Festival each June. At the Three Rivers Regatta in August, boat parades and water-skiing events fill the city's rivers.

Big cities aren't the only places to find fun in the Keystone State. Each August the small town of South Williamsport in north central Pennsylvania is taken over by baseball lovers young and old. Teams from around the country play there in the Little League Baseball World Series.

Fans of professional sports have a lot to choose from in Pennsylvania. The Phillies play baseball in Philadelphia, while the Pirates hit runs for the home crowd in Pittsburgh. The state also has a professional basketball team, the Philadelphia 76ers. Two hockey teams, the Pittsburgh Penguins and the Philadelphia Flyers, as well as two football teams, the Pittsburgh Steelers and the Philadelphia Eagles, play in Pennsylvania.

Young athletes from around the country come to Pennsylvania to play in the Little League Baseball World Series.

For people who enjoy learning about history, Pennsylvania offers a taste of the past at historic sites across the state. Philadelphia's Independence National Historical Park has more history per square foot than almost any other spot in the nation. In just a few downtown blocks, you can tour Independence Hall, visit Congress Hall, see the famous Liberty Bell, and stand at the site of Benjamin Franklin's house.

Elfreth's Alley is Philadelphia's oldest street. Silversmith Philip Syng lived on the street in the 1700s and created the inkwell that was used in the signing of the Declaration of Independence and the U.S. Constitution.

Benjamin Franklin *(center)* is seen here at the historic event of the signing of the Declaration of Independence.

A Few Franklin Firsts

A longtime Philadelphian and a signer of the Declaration of Independence, Benjamin Franklin was also a great inventor. He created a metal rod that stopped lightning bolts from hitting buildings and from starting fires. Franklin's invention of bifocal glasses still helps people see both close up and far away. And versions of the cast-iron Franklin stove, which he first built in 1744, have warmed homes in Pennsylvania and across the country ever since.

Using their feet and non-motorized scooters, Amish boys in Lancaster County head off to school.

Some people might think Lancaster County, west of Philadelphia, looks like a history museum. That's because the area's Amish and Mennonite farmers follow centuries-old traditions. Some still speak the language of their German and Swiss ancestors. For religious reasons, many Amish and some Mennonites choose to live in homes without electricity and to ride in horse-drawn buggies.

Although Pennsylvania is full of traditions and history, it's also packed with new places and ideas. Pittsburgh's Carnegie Institute includes the Museum of Natural History and the Museum of Art. At the Carnegie Science Center, you can walk through a huge model of the human digestive system. With attractions old and new, the Keystone State is a great place to visit—and to call home.

In Langhorne, Pennsylvania *(above)*, kids of all ages play at Sesame Place theme park. Children eagerly pet the animals at the Philadelphia Zoo *(right)*.

THE ENVIRONMENT

Cleaning the Rain

rip, drip, drip. As rain falls each spring, it helps crops grow and flows into streams all over Pennsylvania. But that rain can also hold hidden dangers.

Acid rain refers to rain or other precipitation that is high in acid. Pennsylvania has some of the most acidic rain, snow, sleet, and fog in the country. Acid rain kills fish in lakes in the state's Pocono Mountains and in streams throughout the state. It can cause metals in storage-tank linings to seep into drinking water. And it is slowly eating away at bronze and stone monuments at Gettysburg National Military Park and elsewhere.

Acid rain can be harmful to the people as well as the environment of Pennsylvania.

Pennsylvania needs rainfall to keep its flowers and plants growing, but sometimes the rain contains dangerous levels of acid.

How can rain that looks clean and pure be bad? Scientists have known for a long time that rain falling downwind from industrial areas often contains a lot of acid. They use the **pH** scale to measure how much acid is present. On the pH scale, the lower the number, the higher the level of acid.

Unpolluted rain, for example, contains very little acid and has a pH of about 5.6. During the 1980s, rainfall in Pennsylvania had an average pH of about 4.0, which is about as acidic as cola.

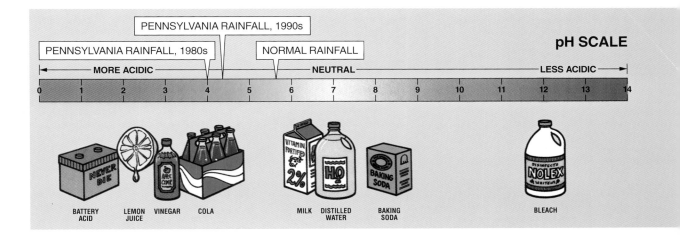

Acid rain is caused when high levels of sulfur dioxide and nitrogen oxide gather in the air. These chemicals come from coal-burning power plants and from car exhaust.

Power plants in the state burn Pennsylvania coal to create electricity. Much of the coal mined in Pennsylvania is high in a chemical called sulfur. When burned, this coal sends poisonous clouds of sulfur dioxide into the atmosphere. Exhaust from cars and trucks contains another chemical, nitrogen oxide, which passes into the air. These chemicals can return to the ground as acid precipitation.

Workers have covered several statues and sculptures in Philadelphia's Fairmount Park with a layer of wax for protection against acid rain.

Pennsylvanians are working to offset damage from acid rain. For example, the state regularly waits to stock trout streams until after snow melts in spring. Snow can have especially high levels of acid. Once acidic snowmelts have run through streams, the water is safer for young fish.

At Gettysburg, monuments are carefully cleaned and covered with a layer of protective wax. Sculptures in Philadelphia's Fairmount Park have also been protected in this way.

Many Pennsylvanians who drink rainwater stored in tanks are testing their water. The acids in acid rain can eat away at metal linings in water tanks and pollute the water. Older tanks are being replaced.

Power plants that use coal for energy expel sulfur dioxide and nitrogen oxide that form acid rain. Since 1995, several power plants in Pennsylvania have been required to reduce emissions to help control air pollution.

But Pennsylvanians are also working to stop acid rain at its source. The state has set tough standards for lowering the amount of sulfur dioxide and nitrogen oxide that power plants and factories can put out. National laws call for less-polluting cars and trucks and set goals for cleaner air across the country.

Smokestacks at many coal-burning power plants in Pennsylvania have been fitted with scrubbers to filter out sulfur dioxide. Scrubbers use powdered limestone and water to absorb pollution before it's released into the air. Plants are also switching to low-sulfur coal.

Attention to the levels of acid in the rain help keep Pennsylvania's streams beautiful.

Reducing the causes of acid rain has created some new problems. When scrubbers at power plants filter out sulfur dioxide, for example, they leave behind tons of waste called sludge. Scrubber sludge is piling up fast in the state's landfills, or places where trash is buried. This can cause the landfills and the areas around them to become polluted.

Despite these setbacks, Pennsylvania's efforts are paying off. The amount of sulfur dioxide produced in the state has decreased 22 percent since 1980.

ACID RAIN

Keeping an Eye on Acid Rain

Each year, Pennsylvania receives some of the most acidic rainfall in the country. Yet scientists have discovered that acid rain causes less damage in Pennsylvania than in some other states.

Why? Geologists have the answer. Most of Pennsylvania's soil and rocks are naturally low in acid. They can absorb the acid in acid rain without great harm. But not all areas in Pennsylvania have this natural ability. In the Pocono Mountains, for example, the thin, rocky soil cannot absorb much acid. Many lakes and streams in the Poconos and throughout the state have been damaged or are in danger of future damage from acid rain.

To keep an eye on conditions in the state, Pennsylvania has set up a monitoring system. Samples of rain and other precipitation taken at monitoring stations are tested for their pH level and for sulfur dioxide and nitrogen oxide. By keeping an eye on acid levels, scientists in Pennsylvania hope to keep on top of the dangers of acid rain. Scientists have found that levels of acid are dropping by up to 25 percent a year.

Nitrogen oxide levels have also been reduced, and the trend continues. By the late 1990s, the average pH of rain in Pennsylvania had gone up to about 4.3. By tackling this threat to the environment head-on, Pennsylvania has become a keystone state in its efforts to take the acid out of acid rain.

Because of the many efforts to reduce pollution, people are able to enjoy area streams.

Weekend tourists are drawn to the Pocono Mountains in northeastern Pennsylvania. Efforts to reduce acid rain in the area's streams and lakes have succeeded in keeping it attractive and welcoming.

ALL ABOUT PENNSYLVANIA

Fun Facts

America's most famous weather forecaster lives in Punxsutawney, Pennsylvania. On February 2 the Punxsutawney groundhog, known as Punxsutawney Phil, comes out of its hole. If the furry forecaster sees its shadow, six more weeks of winter are sure to follow. If the groundhog casts no shadow, spring is just around the corner.

Pennsylvania could be called the state of inventions. Hershey bars, Slinkys, steamboats, and banana splits all got their start in the state.

Punxsutawney Phil, out of his hole, looks for his shadow to determine if spring is on the way.

The **Pennsylvania Dutch in southeastern** Pennsylvania aren't Dutch at all. Their ancestors came from Germany and Switzerland in the late 1600s. They spoke German, or *Deutsch,* as it's called in German. Other settlers misunderstood and thought the newcomers were Dutch.

Pittsburgh hasn't always been spelled with the letter *h* on the end. The h was added on permanently in the early 1900s.

On July 4, 1776, a group of colonists declared themselves free of British rule. This group, called the Fair Play Men, met under a large tree known as the Tiadaghton Elm in northern Pennsylvania to sign their declaration. They didn't know that the Continental Congress was signing the Declaration of Independence in Philadelphia that same day.

Stone carvers finished Pittsburgh's main train station back when Pittsburgh was spelled without its final *h.*

STATE SONG

Pennsylvania's state song was written in 1966. It was
adopted as the official state song in 1990.

PENNSYLVANIA

Written and composed by Edward Khoury and Ronnie Bonner

You can hear "Pennsylvania" by visiting this website:
<http://www.50states.com/songs/penn.htm>

A PENNSYLVANIA RECIPE

Many Philadelphians like to munch on soft pretzels, a twisty snack that's sold on city streets. Legend has it that soft pretzels first appeared in the United States during the 1850s, when a wanderer stopped in Lititz, Pennsylvania. He gave the local baker his recipe for soft pretzels in exchange for a meal. The baker passed the recipe to his assistant, who later started his own pretzel bakery.

SOFT PRETZELS

1 cup warm water
1 package dry active yeast
1½ cups flour
2 tablespoons vegetable oil
½ teaspoon salt

1 ¼ cup flour
4 cups water
2 tablespoons baking soda
coarse salt

1. In large bowl, dissolve yeast in warm water. Let stand for 10 minutes. Then add vegetable oil, salt, and 1½ cups of flour. Stir together until thoroughly combined.
2. Add remaining flour. Knead dough on clean, floured surface for 5 minutes. Then cover with a cloth and let dough rise for 1 hour.
3. Divide dough into 12 equal shapes. Form small balls. Let dough rest for 15 minutes.
4. Roll balls into 18-inch strips. Make pretzel forms. Let pretzels rise for 30 minutes.
5. Ask an adult to help you preheat oven to 475° F.
6. Boil baking soda and water in non-aluminum pot. Ask an adult to help you use tongs to dip each pretzel into boiling water for 1 minute.
7. After pretzels have been dipped in water, place on greased sheetpan. Sprinkle with coarse salt. Bake for 12 minutes. Ask an adult to help you carefully remove pretzels from oven.

HISTORICAL TIMELINE

12,000 B.C.   Native Americans arrive in what later became Pennsylvania.

A.D. 1609   Explorer Henry Hudson sails into Delaware Bay.

1643   Swedes form a colony, called New Sweden, on Tinicum Island, near Philadelphia.

1664   The English take control of the Pennsylvania region from the Dutch, who had taken it from the Swedes.

1681   King Charles II of Britain gives William Penn land west of the Delaware River. Penn founds the colony of Pennsylvania.

1776   The Declaration of Independence is signed in Philadelphia.

1787   Pennsylvania becomes the second state on December 12. The Constitution of the United States is signed in Philadelphia.

1794   The first major hard-surfaced road in the United States is opened between Philadelphia and Lancaster.

Early to mid-1800s   The Underground Railroad succeeds in bringing many slaves to freedom in Pennsylvania and other Northern states.

1834 Canals link Philadelphia and Pittsburgh.

1859 Oil is discovered at Titusville, followed by the creation of the first commercially successful oil well in the United States.

1863 The Battle of Gettysburg takes place and becomes a turning point in the Civil War.

1889 The Johnstown Flood destroys the valley city of Johnstown and kills more than 2,000 people.

1940 The first section of the Pennsylvania Turnpike opens.

1956 The Pennsylvania Turnpike is completed.

1979 An accident occurs at the Three Mile Island nuclear power plant.

1985 Tornadoes cause widespread damage in Pennsylvania.

1993 Doctors at the University of Pittsburgh perform a liver transplant from a baboon to a human.

1998 Republican Tom Ridge is re-elected as Pennsylvania's governor.

OUTSTANDING PENNSYLVANIANS

Louisa May Alcott (1832–1888) authored several children's novels, including the well-known and beloved *Little Women.* Her other books include *Little Men* and *Jo's Boys.* She was born in Germantown, Pennsylvania.

Lloyd Alexander (born 1924) grew up in West Philadelphia, where he bought a copy of *King Arthur and His Knights* at a local bookshop. Inspired by the legends and heroic tales he read as a child, Alexander has created fantasy heroes in over 20 books for children.

Louisa May Alcott

Marian Anderson (1897–1993) began her singing career at the age of six in Philadelphia's Union Baptist church choir. She grew up to be one of the greatest singers of her time, performing in concert and in opera.

Marian Anderson

Nellie Bly (1867–1922) was born in Cochrane Mills, Pennsylvania. Forced to support her family as a young woman, she became a newspaper reporter. Bly became famous when she disguised herself as a disturbed woman and then wrote about her experiences in a mental hospital.

Nellie Bly

Alexander Calder (1898–1976) was born in Lawnton, Pennsylvania, and studied engineering before becoming a sculptor. Calder is famous for his mobiles—sculptures that hang by wires and move with currents of air.

Andrew Carnegie (1835–1919) came to Allegheny, Pennsylvania, from Scotland. Carnegie first worked changing spools of thread in a textile mill. By the end of his career, he ran a steelmaking empire and was one of the richest men in the world.

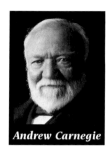

Andrew Carnegie

Rachel Carson (1907–1964), a native of Springdale, was a marine biologist. She brought the topic of dangers to the environment to the general public through her book *Silent Spring*.

Mary Cassatt (1844–1926) was a native of Allegheny City, Pennsylvania, but grew up in Europe. Impressed by the paintings she saw there, Cassatt became the first well-known female impressionist artist.

Mary Cassatt

Chubby Checker (born 1941), a musician, was born Ernest Evans in Philadelphia. While working as a chicken plucker in a poultry shop, he entertained customers so much that the store's owner introduced him to a record producer. Using the name Chubby Checker, he made a song and a dance called "The Twist" popular.

Chubby Checker

Bill Cosby (born 1937) was television's most popular dad during the 1980s in his starring role as Dr. Heathcliff Huxtable on *The Cosby Show*. The Philadelphia native is a well-known writer, comedian, and television producer.

Michael Keaton (born 1951) grew up in Forest Grove, near Pittsburgh. Keaton turned to acting after driving a cab and an ice cream truck for several years. He starred in *Mr. Mom* and *Beetlejuice* before playing Bruce Wayne in *Batman* and *Batman Returns*.

Bill Cosby

Patti LaBelle

Patti LaBelle (born 1944), a singer and actress, was born in Philadelphia. She started her career as a singer with the group Patti LaBelle and the Blue Bells. Since the 1960s, LaBelle has had hit singles such as "The Best Is Yet to Come," and "New Attitude," and "On My Own."

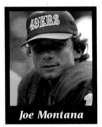

James Michener

James Michener (1907–1997) wrote many historical novels. A native of Doylestown, Michener's first successful novel, *Tales of the South Pacific*, was adapted for the musical *South Pacific*. Michener's books include *Hawaii*, *Space*, *Alaska*, and *Mexico*.

Joe Montana

Joe Montana (born 1956) grew up in Monongahela, Pennsylvania. A football player, Montana earned the nickname the Comeback Quarterback during his years with the San Francisco 49ers. He retired in 1995 as a Kansas City Chief. Montana is an amateur race-car driver and a lecturer.

Arnold Palmer (born 1929) is a Latrobe, Pennsylvania, native. Palmer is the first golfer in history to win the Masters Golf Tournament four times.

Robert E. Peary (1856–1920) may have been the first man to reach the North Pole. The explorer and his team made several attempts to discover the North Pole, and in 1909 they reached it. Peary was born in Cresson, Pennsylvania.

Fred Rogers

Fred Rogers (born 1928) of Latrobe, Pennsylvania, has been asking children "Won't you be my neighbor?" since the 1950s. Host of television's *Mister Rogers' Neighborhood*, Rogers is famous for saying, "There's only one person in the world like you, and I like you just the way you are."

Betsy Ross (1752–1836) was a Philadelphia seamstress, who, according to legend, created the first American flag. In 1776, at George Washington's request, she sewed the first American flag with stars and stripes.

Betsy Ross

James Stewart (1908–1997) was an actor known for his roles as heroic, but ordinary, men. The Indiana, Pennsylvania, native headed to Hollywood in the 1930s. He starred in classic movies such as *It's a Wonderful Life, Mr. Smith Goes to Washington, The Philadelphia Story, Rear Window,* and others.

James Stewart

Henry O. Tanner (1859–1937), of Pittsburgh, studied art in Philadelphia but left for Europe to continue his education and to avoid racism against African Americans. He is best known for his painting of southern blacks and scenes from the Bible.

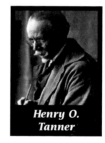

Henry O. Tanner

Jim Thorpe (1886–1953), a Sauk and Fox Native American, studied at the Native American school in Carlisle, Pennsylvania. Thorpe's ability on the football field drew large crowds to Carlisle games, but he is best known for winning gold medals in both the decathlon and pentathlon—two tests of all-around athletic ability—at the 1912 Olympics.

Victoria Van Meter (born 1982) became the youngest female pilot to cross the Atlantic Ocean in 1994, following the path of famous pilot Amelia Earhart. Van Meter was also the youngest female pilot to fly across the continental United States in 1993. She comes from Meadville, Pennsylvania.

August Wilson (born 1945) is a Pulitzer Prize–winning playwright. In *Fences* and other works, Wilson draws on his experiences growing up African American in Pittsburgh.

August Wilson

FACTS-AT-A-GLANCE

Nicknames: Keystone State, Quaker State

Song: "Pennsylvania"

Motto: Virtue, Liberty, and Independence

Flower: mountain laurel

Tree: hemlock

Bird: ruffed grouse

Animal: white-tailed deer

Dog: Great Dane

Insect: firefly

Fish: brook trout

Date and ranking of statehood:
   December 12, 1787, the 2nd state

Capital: Harrisburg

Area: 44,820 square miles

Rank in area, nationwide: 32nd

Average January temperature: 27° F

Average July temperature: 71° F

Pennsylvania's flag features two draft horses, the American eagle, and the state's motto.

POPULATION GROWTH

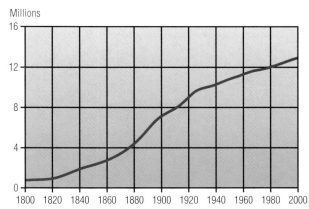

Millions

This chart shows how Pennsylvania's population has grown from 1800 to 2000.

Pennsylvania's state seal was adopted in 1791. It shows a sailing ship, a plow, wheat, and an eagle. The seal also appears on the state's flag.

Population: 12,281,054 (2000 Census)

Rank in population, nationwide: 6th

Major cities and populations: (2000 Census) Philadelphia (1,517,550), Pittsburgh (334,563), Allentown (106,632), Erie (103,717), Upper Darby (81,821)

U.S. senators: 2

U.S. representatives: 19

Electoral votes: 21

Natural resources: anthracite, coal, fertile soil, iron ore, limestone, natural gas, oil, sandstone, shale

Agricultural products: beef cattle, corn, dairy products, greenhouse and nursery products, hay, mushrooms

Manufactured goods: canned mushrooms, chemicals, chocolate, electrical components, electrical equipment, ice cream, industrial machinery, lighting equipment, paint, potato chips, prescription drugs, printed materials, processed foods and beverages, sausages

WHERE PENNSYLVANIANS WORK

Services—67 percent (services include community, social, and personal services; finance, insurance, and real estate; trade; and transportation, communication, and utilities)

Manufacturing—15 percent

Government—11 percent

Construction—5 percent

Agriculture—2 percent

Mining—fewer than 1 percent

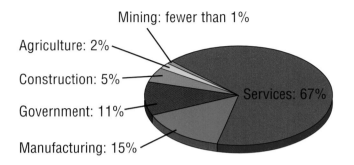

Mining: fewer than 1%
Agriculture: 2%
Construction: 5%
Government: 11%
Manufacturing: 15%
Services: 67%

GROSS STATE PRODUCT

Services—64 percent

Manufacturing—20 percent

Government—10 percent

Construction—4 percent

Agriculture—1 percent

Mining—1 percent

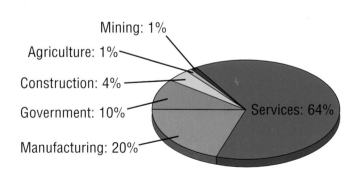

Mining: 1%
Agriculture: 1%
Construction: 4%
Government: 10%
Manufacturing: 20%
Services: 64%

PENNSYLVANIA WILDLIFE

Mammals: black bear, deer, mole, muskrat, opossum, rabbit, raccoon, skunk, squirrel

Birds: gray partridge, ring-necked pheasant, ruffed grouse, wild turkey

Amphibians and reptiles: snakes

Fish: bass, brown trout, carp, chub, pickerel

Trees: ash, aspen, basswood, beech, birch, black cherry, hemlock, hickory, maple, oak, pine, sycamore, tulip tree, walnut

Wild plants: anemone, bloodroot, dog-tooth violet, fern, milkweed, mountain laurel, rhododendron, sundew, wild azalea, wild berries, wild ginger, wild honeysuckle, wintergreen

Rabbit

Raccoon

PLACES TO VISIT

Allegheny National Forest

Located in northwestern Pennsylvania, the Allegheny National Forest offers hiking, biking, and camping near lakes, waterfalls, rivers, and forestland.

Carnegie Museums of Pittsburgh (Carnegie Museum of Art, Carnegie Museum of Natural History, Carnegie Science Center, and the Andy Warhol Museum)

Located in Pittsburgh, the museum system was established by Andrew Carnegie in 1895. The art museum features modern American and European paintings, photographs, sketches, architectural designs, prints, film and video, and sculptures. The natural history museum is famous for its Dinosaur Hall, as well as its natural history exhibits. The science center educates visitors about science and technology through hands-on exhibits. The Andy Warhol Museum contains an extensive collection of Warhol-related items.

Fallingwater, near Uniontown

Frank Lloyd Wright built this famous home onto a waterfall in the Laurel Highlands. The 1935 home is open for tours.

Gettysburg and Gettysburg National Park

Visitors can learn about the battle place that helped the North win the Civil War.

Hawk Mountain Bird Sanctuary, near Allentown

This bird sanctuary, in the Kittatinny Mountains, is a refuge for birds of prey. The sanctuary has a visitor center and hiking trails.

Hershey

Visitors to Hershey can experience several attractions, including HersheyPark, Hershey Chocolate World, Hershey Gardens, Hershey Museum, Hershey Theater, and Founders Hall.

Independence National Historical Park, Philadelphia

This park includes Independence Hall, Congress Hall, and the Liberty Bell. Visitors can see where the Declaration of Independence was signed and learn about the founding of the United States.

Longwood Gardens, near Philadelphia

One of the most spectacular gardens in the world, Longwood Gardens in Chester County feature indoor and outdoor gardens, an open-air theater, and fountains.

Pennsylvania Dutch country

Amish people, called "Pennsylvania Dutch," live a traditional lifestyle in Lancaster County in southeastern Pennsylvania. Visitors can ride a horse-and-buggy through an Amish community. Other attractions include an amusement park, covered bridges, and many museums.

Fallingwater

ANNUAL EVENTS

Mummers' Parade, Philadelphia—*January*

Groundhog Day Celebration, Punxsutawney—*February*

Chocolate Festival, Hershey—*February*

Three Rivers Arts Festival, Pittsburgh—*June*

Pennsylvania Renaissance Faire, Cornwall—*July to October*

Freedom Festival, Philadelphia—*July*

Little League Baseball World Series, South Williamsport—*August*

Pittsburgh Three Rivers Regatta, Pittsburgh—*August*

Bean Soup Festival, McClure—*September*

Reenactment of Washington Crossing the Delaware, Washington Crossing Historic Park, Philadelphia—*December*

Kwanzaa celebration, Philadelphia—*December–January*

LEARN MORE ABOUT PENNSYLVANIA

BOOKS

General

Fradin, Dennis Brindell. *Pennsylvania.* Chicago: Children's Press, 1996.

Heinrichs, Ann. *Pennsylvania.* Chicago: Children's Press, 2000. For older readers.

Whitehurst, Susan. *The Colony of Pennsylvania.* New York: The Rosen Publishing Group, 2000. Describes the history of Pennsylvania during the colonial period of the United States up to the American Revolution.

Special Interest

Burford, Betty. *Chocolate by Hershey: A Story about Milton S. Hershey.* Minneapolis: Carolrhoda Books, Inc., 1994. Tells the story of Milton S. Hershey's life and his world-famous chocolate business.

Currie, Stephen. *We Have Marched Together.* Minneapolis: Lerner Publications Company, 1997. For older readers. Currie describes the conditions of Philadelphia's child workers in the nineteenth and early twentieth centuries. The book also tells of Mother Jones's fight to end child labor.

Ransom, Candice F. *Listening to Crickets: A Story about Rachel Carson.* Minneapolis: Carolrhoda Books, Inc., 1999. Ransom tells the story of Rachel Carson, a marine biologist who brought environmental concerns to light in the United States with her 1962 book *Silent Spring*.

Streissguth, Tom. *Mary Cassatt: Portrait of an American Impressionist*. Minneapolis: Carolrhoda Books, Inc., 1999. Tells the story of Mary Cassatt's life and includes many color photos of her paintings.

Fiction

Cummings, Priscilla. *Autumn Journey*. New York: Cobblehill Books/Dutton, 1997. Will and his family move from Baltimore, Maryland, to Will's grandfather's farm in Pennsylvania. Will wounds a goose on his first hunting trip. He nurses the goose back to health, but then he has to face his grandfather's death.

Freeman, Martha. *The Year My Parents Ruined My Life*. New York: Holiday House, 1997. Kate and her family move from California to a small town in Pennsylvania. Kate's life is turned upside down until she learns to accept her new home.

Oatman High, Linda. *A Stone's Throw from Paradise*. Grand Rapids, MI: Eerdmans Books for Young Readers, 1997. To have a break from her new stepfamily, Lizzie visits her grandmother in Pearly Gates, Pennsylvania. Lizzie learns about the Amish as well as about her mother and herself.

Walker, Paul Robert. *Head for the Hills!* New York: Random House, 1993. This short novel allows readers to experience the great Johnstown flood.

Woodruff, Elvira. *Dear Austin: Letters from the Underground Railroad.* New York: Alfred A. Knopf, 1998. Through letters he writes to his brother Austin, Levi tells of his experience traveling through Pennsylvania and helping runaway slaves on the Underground Railroad.

WEBSITES

PA PowerPort
<www.state.pa.us>
An official state website with information on living and working in the state and up-to-date links to government offices and news media.

100% Pure Pennsylvania
The state travel and tourism bureau's site features outdoor activities, arts and entertainment, attractions, lodging, and historic places.

Historic Philadelphia
<www.ushistory.org/tour/>
This site offers a virtual tour of the many historic sites in the City of Brotherly Love, along with an index that takes you directly to the spot of your choice.

The Philadelphia Inquirer
<http://inq.philly.com/content/inquirer/home/>
Check out this daily newspaper for online coverage of Philadelphia and Pennsylvania news.

PRONUNCIATION GUIDE

Allegheny (al-uh-GAY-nee)

Amish (AHM-ish)

Appalachian Plateau
(ap-uh-LAY-chuhn pla-TOH)

Conestoga (kahn-uh-STOH-guh)

Deutsch (doytch)

Lenape (luh-NAH-pee)

Monongahela (muh-non-guh-HEE-luh)

Pocono (POH-kuh-noh)

Punxsutawney (puhnk-suh-TAW-nee)

Susquehanna (suhs-kwuh-HAN-uh)

Susquehannock (suhs-kwuh-HAN-uhk)

Deer thrive in the forests of Pennsylvania.

GLOSSARY

acid rain: any precipitation that is high in acid. Acid rain occurs when precipitation passes through an atmosphere polluted with sulfur dioxide and nitrogen oxide.

colony: a territory ruled by a country some distance away

constitution: the system of basic laws or rules of a government, society, or organization; the document in which these laws or rules are written

Great Lakes: a chain of five lakes in Canada and the northern United States. They are Lakes Superior, Michigan, Huron, Erie, and Ontario.

immigrant: a person who moves to a foreign country and settles there

Latino: a person who either came from or has ancestors from Latin America

nuclear power: a way of producing energy and electricity using atoms, the tiny building blocks of the universe

pH: a measure of the level of acid in a substance

precipitation: rain, snow, sleet, and hail

radioactive: giving off rays of energy called radiation, which happens when atoms of certain elements change to other elements

turnpike: a highway on which a toll, or fee, is collected from drivers at various points along the route

Underground Railroad: a system of escape routes that helped slaves get from the South to the North or Canada, where they would be free

INDEX

PHOTO ACKNOWLEDGMENTS

Cover photos by © Joe McDonald/Corbis (left) and © Leif Skookfors/Corbis (right); © David Muench/Corbis, pp. 2-3; © W. Cody/Corbis, p. 3; © Karlene Schwartz, pp. 4 (detail), 7 (detail), 17 (detail) 39 (detail) 51 (detail); Endless Mountains Visitors Bureau, p. 6; Mae Scanlon, pp. 7, 11, 42 (left), 59; PresentationMaps.com, pp. 1, 8, 9, 44; © Sally Weigand, pp. 10, 50 (left), 54, 56, 58; Chester County Tourist Bureau, pp. 12, 17; Erie Area Chamber of Commerce, pp. 13, 52; PA Dutch Convention & Visitors Bureau, p. 14; Sylvia Schlender, p. 15; Jerry Hennen, p. 16; Library Company of Philadelphia, pp. 18, 21; Library of Congress, pp. 20, 33, 35, 48, 67 (top), 69 (top); Mr. & Mrs. Meyer P. Potamkin, p. 22; © North Wind Pictures, p. 23; IPS, pp. 24, 31, 66 (second from bottom); Thomas P. Benincas, Jr., pp. 25, 26; © Mary A. Root/Root Resources, p. 27; Print & Picture Collection, Free Library of Philadelphia, p. 29; MG-219 Commercial Museum Collection, PA State Archives, p. 30; Lehigh County Historical Society, p. 32 (left); Paul Witt, p. 32 (right); California Museum of Photography, Keystone-Mast Collection, U. of CA Riverside, p. 34; Urban Archives, Temple Univ., Philadelphia, PA, p. 36; PA Turnpike Commission, p. 37; © James Blank/Root Resources, pp. 38, 47; © Buddy Mays/Corbis, p. 39; Betty Groskin, p. 40; Harrisburg-Hershey-Carlisle Tourism & Convention Bureau, p. 41; John R. Patton, pp. 42 (right), 43, 49, 55; Colin P. Varga, p. 45; © Elsa/Allsport, p. 46; Bucks County Tourist Comm., p. 50 (right); PA Dept. of Environmental Resources, pp. 51, 57 (photo by Paul Zeph); © Reuters NewMedia Inc./Corbis, p. 60; Michael Medford, p. 61; Tim Seeley, pp. 63, 71, 72; Courtesy of the Louisa May Alcott Memorial Association, p. 66 (top); Station KSTP, Minneapolis, p. 66 (second from top); Portrait of the Artist (detail), Metropolitan Museum of Art, Bequest of Edith H. Proskauer, 1975, p. 67 (second from top); Hollywood Book & Poster, pp. 67 (second from bottom, bottom), 68 (top, bottom); Frank Capri/SAGA/Archive Photos, p. 68 (second from top); San Francisco 49ers, p. 68 (second from bottom); Photofest, p. 69 (second from top); Henry Ossawa Tanner Papers (detail), Archives of American Art, Smithsonian Institute, p. 69 (second from bottom); University of Pittsburgh, p. 69 (bottom); Jean Matheny, p. 70 (top); © Joe McDonald/Corbis, pp. 73 (both), 80; © Shmuel Thaler, p. 75